His Ear Bends Low

THE POETRY OF JULIE PACK

His Ear Bends Low
Copyright © 2021 Julie Pack
ALL RIGHTS RESERVED WORLDWIDE

MANIFEST
PUBLICATIONS

ISBN: 978-1-951280-13-0

Scriptures marked NIV are taken from the NEW INTERNATIONAL VERSION (NIV): Scripture taken from THE HOLY BIBLE, NEW INTERNATIONAL VERSION ®. Copyright© 1973, 1978, 1984, 2011 by Biblica, Inc.™. Used by permission of Zondervan

Cover Design: Don Patton
Proofreading by Susan Williams

Dedication

This book is dedicated to my J-Pack family, aka Joshua, Jared, and Jace.

May you always remember that you are seen, heard, and loved by a LIVING GOD.

Contents

#	Poem	Page
p	*Preface*	i
1	Today	1
2	Caribou	3
3	Renaissance Man	5
4	Depression	8
5	Being	10
6	Elapse	13
7	Wonders	15
8	Think	17
9	Seeker's Come	19
10	Chaos	21
11	Labyrinth	22
12	Futuristic	24
13	Catacombs	27
14	Once	29
15	Unforgettable	32
16	Tender Now	33
17	Tenderness	35
18	Skilled Musician	37

19	Face the Light	40
20	North Wind	42
21	Deep Pools	43
22	Silence	45
23	Fidelity	47
24	Circle	48
25	Paper Mache	51
26	Conquest	53
27	Gale	55
28	Show Me	56
29	Holy Fire	58
30	Habits	60
31	Romanced by Him	63
32	The Road Less Travelled	68
33	Rise	70
34	Come Home	72
35	True Beauty	74
36	His Time	75
37	Prepare the Forces	76
38	Quiet Your Heart	77
39	Enjoying Winter	79
40	Missing You	80
41	Taken Away	82
42	Child Eyes	84

43	Rise Again	85
44	Imagine	86
45	Hike	87
46	Look	88
47	Spin	90
48	You Saw Me	91
49	Fools Gold	92
50	Drink	93
51	Sail On	94
52	Holy Hill	95
	Finding the Way Home	96
	Acknowledgements	99
	About the Author	101

Preface

Many years ago, I was part of a program called *Masters Commission* in Illinois. As a second-year student, I was placed on the mission team and learned a lot about sharing my faith with people from other cultures, backgrounds, and religions. My most memorable experience, however, did not take place within the walls of the school.

Each team member was given a religion to study. I was assigned the religion of Buddhism. I really didn't know much about this religion, so I began my research at a local bookstore. I quickly grew tired of looking through books on the subject. Instead, I began searching for Buddhist temples nearby. When I found one, I was a little bit nervous about going there. Before I lost my nerve, I knocked on the door. And a Buddhist monk answered. But unfortunately, he didn't speak English and no one else at that temple did either. Therefore, he sent me to a neighboring temple.

When I arrived at this monastery, I was met at the door by a delightful monk wearing a smile and a bright orange robe. He was well-versed in several languages, spoke perfect English, and was extremely intelligent. I told him that I wanted to learn about the Buddhist religion and asked if he had time to talk with me. He was excited to do so! Apparently, he frequently spoke at the local colleges about Buddhism.

As we entered the temple together, I noticed a large golden statue of Buddha. There was incense burning, food offerings, and flowers lying all around the statue. I asked him if Buddha ever came to eat the food. He started laughing, almost to the point of tears! "No, no," he said. "Buddha is dead. We wait a few days, and then we eat the food." He then went on to tell me how many times a day that he and the other monks pray to Buddha. I asked him if Buddha ever hears his prayers. Again, he laughed! How silly he must have thought I was. "No, no, Buddha doesn't hear," he stated, "Buddha is dead."

I thought this was very interesting! So, I explained, "Well, I serve a living God, who not only hears my prayers but answers me as well." To this he replied, "I must know more about this God." This began a great friendship that lasted the rest of my time in Illinois.

I tell you this story because I want to make sure that you as a reader of my poems are clear about this: I know that the world has many versions of who God is but these poems are for the LIVING GOD. I do not petition a deaf or mute idol. I call out to Jesus who is the way, the truth, and the life. There is no way to the Living God except through Jesus. (See John 14:6.) And as you read these poems, don't take my word for it - ask Him for yourself. Ask Jesus to reveal Himself to you. Cry out to Him, and He will answer you.

This book of poems is written for people who are seeking God, seeking the truth, and seeking the life that God has for you. Keep seeking and don't stop! You will find what you're searching for if you keep on seeking!

This book is for the prodigals who have wandered away from God. You know the truth but feel you've strayed too far off the path. It's okay. Come home. Many are waiting for your return but none more than Jesus. All of Heaven will rejoice over your return. It doesn't matter what you have done. Just come home.

This book is for the saints. No matter how deep your relationship with Jesus may be, you can always go deeper. He sings over you and has so much in store for you. Regardless of your age or ability, He still has marvelous plans for those who love Him.

Lastly, this book is for the children. The Father loves you and takes great delight in watching you grow, and He enjoys all the little moments of your life. You are never too young to take His hand.

For everyone who will read this book, I hope that you enjoy these poems and know as you read them that *HIS EAR BENDS LOW* for you the same way it does for me.

Today

The Presence is indeed a present if we live in the moment of now.

Too often my mind leaves my body, and I go off to another land…

Lost in the dreams of possibilities.

I long to be present in the everyday…

To fully feel the crunch of the fall leaves underneath my feet,

To take in the essence of the ebony tree,

To enjoy the laughter of small children.

Where do my thoughts take me?

Up the rivers of the past and light years beyond today.

Now it is healthy and quite beneficial to take time for proper reflection and surely there is no harm found in the hopes of future days;

But how much time is wasted in reminiscing or worst yet… fear and regret.

My grievances for untold desires; my pity for forsaken dreams; my tears for skeletons that no one will ever see; my sorrowful moans for the wounds I've created.

Let it lay buried deep… rise and take flight again.
My smile for tomorrow, my relief in being heaven bound, my joy for the future… but what about now?

To feel every moment,
Here is where I am…
Where I'm meant to be.
As I walk, I look around and take in the fullness of my stride.
Freshness upon face and a glow in the air,
The brightness of the clouds and the redness of the trees…
Such beauty and wonder were almost passed by.
The morning almost tainted,
But I made the choice… the choice to be present… the choice to enjoy.
Such contentment is meant for every creature…
The fondness of simplicity in an all too complex of a world.
Somehow, I must hold on to this key of simple truth.
May it resonate deep within my being.

Tomorrow is not promised, and yesterday has gone away,
But now is the time to live, to thrive, to bless…
Not in hopes or fears, but in praise and utter adoration of today.

Caribou

While the complex tendencies of the everyday surround me, I cannot help but chuckle to myself.

The wild roaming fields of peace are a delight and pleasure to much more than the caribou.

Sometimes, my feet long to take my soul on a journey beyond the borders and horizons that I have currently seen.

To feel the caress of the northern wind, to taste the spice of the eastern markets, to be enticed by the rawness of the south, to experience the latest trends of the emerging west…

To be civilized and proper, to be a merchant and a tourist, to be a blessing and a beacon of hope, to be poor and wild, yet completely content…

Whether bounding up a hill or sailing on smooth waters…

Whether in laughter or in mourning…

May my heart be content in the fact that it is His.

Freedom to roam and freedom to stay…

Whether in riches or in rags,

His love is still extravagant.

Whether in chains or roaming free,

In weakness and in strength,

It is still extravagant!

Love me as I fly
Love me as I land
Love me as I fail
Love me as I succeed

Accomplishment...
Definition...
It's all found here
In the rays of true light.
It can be experienced anywhere at any given time.
All you need is the desire, the heart, the cry.

Imagination is in vain if the motives are not pure...
My petition is one for purity: to remove any moldy condition.
After all, true amazement is not found in the rolling of any hills
Or in the beauty of any physical design.
It is found in the innermost place of intimacy with one's own Creator...
In the sheer wonder of being loved by such an incredible being...
Pour it out and shine it down.
The reward for seeking is a treasure found!

Renaissance Man

Dispersion of stolen goods fortified beneath the city gates

Dragons guard the entrance

Their breath scares the locals and transcends the valley with fear

Operations cease as the reckoning begins

Hope pierces the walls of even the coldest of dwellings

A maverick of the times demands justice for the people

Together, they believe that another world is possible

Rigidness is slowly softened as the dancers begin to play their tambourines

An essence of peace begins to pierce the air

An ambiance of joy quakes in the wind

A loving remembrance takes form in even the hardest of hearts

The reflections of the past break forth to the knowledge of the day

A reckless man now sees the errors of his ways
Truth be told and truth be known
Savageness resides in us all
Unspoken sin blackens our minds

Then, He came
He shattered the brokenness of our lives
He came on clouds of thunder
The love displayed was so intense that it ended in His death
It was so powerful that even Hades could not hold its grip
His love was so strong that it snapped the cords of injustice and set free all who loved Him from the snares of death

Overpowering emotion overcame even the cruelest of men

Uncharted territories are now open for exploration
Allow not your mind the leisure of casual reminiscence
It is time for the present to overtake the moment of now
Horizons expanded by the breath of the Dove
Future outlook is exceedingly good

Impossibilities now become possible
Never doubt what has been hidden in your being

Deny yourself not the fellowship of your family
Beckon hell's doors no more
Flirtation is deadly when it is not clean
Overtaken by my mind, my soul tarries in the balance
Once given over, my life will never be the same
Designed to live and die in Him
I will cleave no longer to this world of sin

Renaissance Man, take me home again
Renaissance Man, take me back to where I began
To run this race no longer alone…
To run this race until I reach home

Depression

Depression seeps in to wither the hope of triumph. It pierces the light and dulls the senses. It steals tomorrow, and harps upon the mistakes of yesterday. It forces the strong down, mocking them in the mind. All joy becomes contaminated and lifeless. Loving displays appear fake and even conniving. Victory and peace seem so far away though I was certain of their presence only moments ago.

How is this travesty allowed to play itself out? Where is my sword? My armor has been collecting dust in the corner. Wounded, I rise to brush it off and place it around my chest. Please my Lord will You hear my cry? I need the strength to wage this war. I need the strength for what is in store. Build me up so that I cannot be torn down. Build me up so I can take this ground. I need Your life; come breathe on me. I need Your life, LORD, come set me free. I am tired of striving; I cannot go on. So, I ask for grace to see me thru. I ask for grace until my time is due.

Too many promises made in vain. Too many tears shed without any gain. Hear my prayers Lord! Please come and set me free. I'm so lonely that my chest has caved in. I'm so lonely Lord. Please steer me clear of sin. My mind has been tortured for far too long. I'm weary of singing this same old song. Teach me how to hold on to my joy. Teach me how, Lord, to truly enjoy; everything that You have for me. Oh, teach me Lord how to just rest and be. I cannot control my analytical mind. I cannot let go and leave my past far behind. I'm weary of grieving; it has been far too long.

Teach me Lord to sing the victory song!

BEING

The blows have been mighty
Given bruises defined in the attack
Merciless hits upon the head as well as on the mind
The abused one forgets their worth
Into the shadows they hide
Silence feels safe
Emptiness becomes a false blanket of security
Frowns can even look like smiles
Slowly they creep from their caverns…
But the distance is still evident to the open eye
How far is too far?
It depends on who is taking the journey

You see my **LOVER** tires not
His heart beats onward
Hades could not hold Him nor was it too far for Him to travel
This is in fact where we first met
Rather, where I first became aware that He was always there with me

Broken pieces need more than glue

Elmer's simply cannot do the trick

We try to piece ricocheted jaded parts back together again

He simply blows His breath and new parts are formed

Now, I am no scientist and find myself ignorant and feeble in many facets of ways

But I must say with boldness and clarity of thought

That I know all that is worth knowing

That I have all that is worth having

And I learn all that could possibly be worth learning

From one simple thing

Being

Not being alone or with others or being "one" with the universe…

But in just **being with Him**

Quietness, softness, peacefulness, gracefulness, and love

All await me in the being of Him

I hear a call…

A call to exposure of the treasures and the trash

Let Him blow upon you for His breath formed the heavens

Set sail upon His wings of freedom…

Can you hear Him now calling out?

"Come out, come out, my precious bride!
I'm waiting for you on the other side.
Wounded warrior, come. I'm here to set you free.
Wounded warrior, come. The prize is to just rest and be."

Selah

Elapse

The elapse of time escapes my memory once again.

Fragments of distilled thoughts target the very essence of my being.

Uncharted waters being met by the revealer of destiny.

Unspoken words are heard clearly through the eyes that reflect one's soul.

Little is hidden when hearts are laid bare.

Feverish dreams ride us into the beckoning of tomorrow.

Soft ambers burn thick throughout the night.

Faithful justice, vindicator of all truth, stand strong now beyond the willows of the sunset.

An onset of flavors rush amongst the pores of my skin.

Pleasant fragrance draws me in.

Sweet lullabies carry me home once again…

Safe inside the vault of my Creator's heart.

Here, I find rest for the embarkment of a new journey.

Fresh, vexing, and full of life.

Courage swiftly rises within as I engage the present tense of speech…

And begin walking in the midst of every moment.

Moving past the space of hours…

No longer floating but becoming seemingly grounded.

Rooted deep, the tree flourishes with strength and vivacious beauty,

It feeds the hungry and clothes the weak.

Travelers come from miles around to sit beneath its shade

And listen to the leaves as they blow in the gentle wind.

It will stand strong throughout various trials and storms.

It will lend its fruit, and its juice will satisfy the thirsty.

No man can cut down this tree!

It was planted for a specific purpose and will only be uprooted by its planter

When the appointed moment has arrived.

Wonders

Wonders forsake not the curious mind
Open to concepts forbidden by time

Lasting results foreshadowed in the release of precision
Conditions remarked by the valley of decision

Up forcing winds travel homeward bound
No need to elaborate on the profound

Endlessness begins with the curve of a smile
Tides rise and fall as the sun beats its dial

Courage is fitting only for a king
The rest are just puppets being pulled on a string

Wayward thoughts held captive by the splendid light
A heart beats open that loves with all it's might

Forgotten encouragement floods the mind
Whimsical displays leave the past far behind

Moments of bliss engraved in the soul
A feeling of oneness that makes one whole

Begotten by Spirit, poured out in the flesh
Birthed from a womb where the two at once meshed

The Father spoke and it was to be
Everything created for all to see

So, gaze at the wonder and hold fast a stare
For this is a world that we can all share

THINK

The pandemonium of unleashed desire boils inside my veins
The utter chaos of forbidden passion resides deep within
The burden of loving one beyond your reach
It feels like a marauder is being placed upon my very soul

Humbling, yet frightening, I battle feelings I thought only a pagan could possess
I realize my own humanness despite the power of purity
What a fractal display is the mind of man
It cannot be understood in a few simple words
Who am I to even begin to define it?

Hope is what I cling to, for it is all I have
Hope in what is holy, righteous, and true
Hope in being rewarded for a diligence of seeking

Profound insight keeps me afloat
Without it surely, I would be found below the sea anchored deep in shame

Running this race demands all you possess
Nothing can be kept for the sake of yourself
To love your life is to lose it
To give your life is to gain it back again

Intense words of no subtle intent
Think, meditate, discover –
Not only who you are, but who you were created to be

Seekers Come

Seekers, come
Seekers, ride
Seekers, fly
Come invite the wind – long for the fire

No longer fearful of the ominous threatening clouds
No longer perplexed by the dull dawning of complacency
The feeble become the audacious
Taking the rivers of life in stride
Surfing upon waves of joy
Recognizing the truth

We were not created to hide, but to thrive
Realizing that we were made auspicious in the sight of the Most High
Loved and highly favored
Vibrant and beaming with life and purpose
To live –
To live well and simply

Hiding not what has been given, but exposing it for all to see
All pride is masked behind jargon that few can understand
But all understand true beauty –
All understand the purity of love

From the throne to the earth –
From the throne to the earth –
May we live to bring heaven here
Wherever we walk, rivers will flow
Ask not only for yourself –
Ask for others

Bend your knee and let your petition be known
On earth as it is in heaven –
On earth as it is in heaven

Chaos

Nothing in this wasteland of desolate dreams is for me.
Disenchantments are soon followed by harsh reality.
People flying by pretending to be gods of their own domain.
Their glass houses will soon shatter.
Shards pierce the flesh, but the dead don't realize they are bleeding.
Alive ones wander, trying to resuscitate fragments of truth
Nestled deep within the human species.

Predicted predators are yesterday's past victims.
Left unhealed and unwhole, their wounds fester.
Their anger boils over into others causing the spread of disease.

Answers to all questions flourish in the light of the Divine.
May your eyes be open wide to the astonishment of true deity –
Not to be fathomed or held,
But to be embraced and loved.

Labyrinth

A labyrinth of complexity forms in the average mind.
The cross stands as the only true emblem of peace.
Often sheer unhindered emotion gives way to the impalement of one's own soul.

Disputed revelation often breaks way to even more precious treasures –
Jewels that sparkle well with life
Deep seeded wonders.

Dignitaries plunder the physical and sometimes spiritual wealth of the masses.
Clothed in false humility while asserting their own agendas.
Who's to say what is righteous?
All is found in the pages of the good Book.
Life spins around in circular motions.
Escapades must surely all come to an end.
Escape the definition of the worldly norm!

Clandestine meetings of grace,
Forever, they will radiate with HIS joy.

The perennial beauty of those who are defined in HIM.

Crossroads will always bring challenge throughout our lives.

Head on collisions with the enemy

No more snakes allowed in this garden.

Gentle giants, come and wage your war.

Stillness overcomes the anxious heart.

The inner cries have been heard.

Peace becomes me…

Overshadowed now by the mighty eagle's wings.

FUTURISTIC

Futuristic procession of translucent essence.
Peaceful abundance forever radiating.
You will find no mild inconsistencies here.

Zoned out for perfection…
Uphill we march…
Onward!
The sun blisters our lips, but still, we trek…
Mission clearly stated.

No time for mournful good-byes.
Stay on track and focus your eye like a flint.
No weight will be required that you will not be given the strength to carry.

Charlatans will soon be revealed and dealt with by death.
The anomaly of this world are the saints in the next…
Forgiven and bestowed upon.
Wonderful revelation brings sweetness to parched and barren souls…
Lovely pilgrims journey home.

Packed with precision and armed with might,

Percussion rifts throughout the valleys.

Its sound is astounding.

Ripples of hope enter the hearts of the weak.

Escalades of fever come into the sleeping little town.

Silence is taken over by stimulation.

Fictitious characters have infiltrated the average man's life…

No longer in his world but living in the fantasy of someone else's.

How tragic is this place to be in?

We have allowed idols to determine our days.

Subliminal messages slowly drain the mind… corrupt the spirit.

Where are the princes?

Where are the kings and queens?

This should not be allowed in our Lord's land.

How is this justifiable or even permissible?

Sadness overtakes the Creator's heart.

He has purposed so much more than this.

Instead of asking His will, many gorge themselves on the profanity of filth,

Steering clear of anything that may convict them in any way.

Perishable goods soon fade away leaving one hungry and very alone.

As the saints continue their march, the sleepy little town starts to slowly rise.

Some rise out of anger…

Some rise to join in the march.

Truth does not allow anyone to lie down.

Current devotion draws them out of their beds.

They stumble from their darkness out into the light.

One question is asked, and each must only answer for themselves…

Whom will you serve?

Choose this day whom you will serve!

Catacombs

The catacombs of our lives weave us along an interesting journey to be sure

Unspoken relics of the heart burst forth upon the new horizon

Steadfast leadership of the most benign warrior King one could possibly imagine

Radiant displays of a Lord worth knowing

Crossroads of the Master Weaver's plan

All for One and One for all

The epitaph of our lives matters not in this world but is vital in the next

Spoken from the mouths of angels…

The truth of who we really are

Not in the flukiness of our chances or our will

He grounds us deep

Sets our minds and hearts in motion

To breathe Him in is to be complete

Motions of the earth will one day cease to be

Human parasitic nature will be no more

Kindness will overtake mankind

The lion will lie down with the lamb

All will find rest

Need not wait until that day for the peace within

All around, may we spin

Basking in the fluid flow of Him

Once

Once a kettle called the pot black
Once a prophet turned to scream
The terror of one tormented by their own soul
To admit no wrong is danger
To force others to see…. impossible

How rare is the gift of reason
Fallen knees lead to grand results
Splendor is fitting only for royalty
Amazement is most fascinating when it's at one's own self
Gifted speaker please keep silent!
I long for no false grandeur or schemes
Purity without virtue isn't purity at all but defilement
See the speck, but focus on the plank
Reality bites the dust, once again

You can run, but you can't hide…
Not from you or from Him
The verdict lies in the design
Who can accomplish what was purposed?

Can you or I?
Only in our pride

Sin sets free when it's brought out into the light
Let's march forward without anger on display
The closer we get to freedom the more our soul's cry
You can taste it but not grasp it
It's not for you to steal
Some goods can't be taken but only developed over time

Ask yourself this question... where can you go to hide?
To hide from your Creator... now that's a funny game
A game that you will surely lose
Let us ride together until the dusk meets the dawn
You're never too late while you still have a choice
It's not over - It has only begun
Let's play the game of life together
Not everyone will win, but all will play

Whose side are you on?
Let us roam this world with dignity and strength that none can take
The redeemed prostitute became the most beautiful of all brides
That's a story worth noting...
A tale worth telling

So let us sit by the fire to conspire and reflect
What brought us this far and what will take us even farther still?

What is your tale?
Sit
I'll listen with eyes wide open and ears eager to hear
I hear a story of tragedy, love, and despair
Hopelessness was never meant to cling to

Come, it's time to bow our heads in reverence and in utter adoration
May His peace stay with you always…
No matter the valleys or the hills

Unforgettable

Superstitious pragmatic thoughts

Learning the art of approaching life tacitly

Knowing the truth but being quick to acquiesce when necessary

Throughout this journey, there have been many turmoils, trials, and distractions

Still, for the most part, I have remained unscathed

His hand has been upon me since the beginning of time

His thoughts of me too many to number

Before terra firma was, there He was

Silent, but not at all still

Created beings – we were made for His delight

How sad His heart must be at times

The unforgettable One that is often forgotten

Purge the heart of all defilement

May we see purely once again

Tender Now

Sharp shards of stained steel glass

Charades of the best blues dancers you'd ever see

Whimsical chariots of raining fire

Sweet crevasses being filled that you never even knew were empty

Beginning and ending all twirled with mixed motion into ONE sound

For life and liberty of the mind and of the spirit

Clutching only leads to death by suffocation

Up one side and down another

If love only knew when to give up

Horrific, yet astounding displays of counterfeit caresses

Here we go

Ride into the storm and not away from it

For the victory is in the midst and not found on the sidelines

Battles won in praises far above the atmosphere

Tender now

Tender now little seed

Tender now

Tender now little seed

Tender now

Tender now little seed

Soon, you will be a fortress for the trees

Tenderness

Tenderness exposing the hidden dilemmas
Our greatest fears laid bare for all to see
Will they still love me when they know?

Beaten down by enemies of the mind
Forgetting the grace that lingers, just waiting for my reach
Bestowed upon by the most gracious of lords and lovers

Westward bound, my soul cries out for home
A place of light and of life
A place of solace, peace, and forgiveness
A place of refreshing springs and jubilant creatures
A place of ultimate rest

Creator God, look down on me
Open my vaulted heart that I may see
He speaks the truth and tells no lie
He holds me close that I may never die

Once poured out was His life given for all

If you listen closely, you will hear the call

May we ask for a timely release

Where the voice of HIM remains and all others will cease

Skilled Musician

Skilled musician, lend me not your tune
I long for no worship of the silver-lined moon
Give it to me real; give it to me raw
Out of the depths I cry and merely the senses you draw

Father in heaven, please hear my plea
I wait for the presence of Your glory to see
Before me is vacant, behind me is dross
I hunger for the full revelation of the cross
I know that the whole thing I could not bear
But perhaps just another piece for me can You spare?

I pant for the crumbs found fallen from Your table
It is You who have made me strong; it is You who have made me able
Like a wild stallion fighting with pride to be free
You looked and saw the useful and humble servant that was to be
With time and training and patience as the key

You will tame my temper and my will
To endure and enjoy all You have for me

I can't comprehend the seasons past
I still don't understand why human love does not last
But You cover my tears with the blood of the Lamb
You're forcing the river to become a stable dam

Purge my heart of the ugliness inside
Teach me how to truly live – in You I will reside
Feed me with a passion for Your throne
Help me to see that for my sins I cannot atone

Back to the basics and stripping the strife
It is You my Lord I want to control my life
I'm tired of sickness for no fair gain
I'm weary of sorrow keeping me sane

Birth in me a joy that will not cease
Precious Holy Spirit, I ask for a release
A release of Your standards, a dimension of Your peace
Thank You Lord for these treasures I find
Grant me grace to hold them in my heart and not only in my mind

Breath of Life, I surrender now

Breath of Life, show me how

How to love You the best way that I can

To live each day to delight You and not to please any man

Face the Light

Liaison, come and speak to me now
My mind is so cluttered that it does not allow my heart to speak
Confusion overwhelms me
I have so many fears
Of fate, of failure, of love
Take time to unwind
To hear
To listen
Not to redefine or interpret but just to hear in peaceful wonder

Love and lust are as opposite as night and day
One takes and abandons
The other stays and continues to love
No one is perfect
No one is righteous
Why then do I feel so unworthy of anything good?
I sabotage myself before anyone else can
I run from my own shadow
Pounce on my own weaknesses

Why is it that self is the one that drives the mind most mad?

You'd think by now one would understand their own mind, but it puzzles me still

High class, low class

It affects us all

Fear, unbelief, misery, and foolish pride

Up again with my back to the sun

When will I realize that freedom will come only when I face the light?

NORTH WIND

Dare not speak for fear of frivolous dreams
Compensation will not be met with regret
Stillness overcomes the hardness of my heart
Peaceful freedom flow
Shalom, may rest be yours
Wake in the morning with refreshing song
North wind blow
"North wind blow… upon my garden"[1]
May its fragrance draw my lover nigh to me

Forbidden fruit suddenly blessed by Hands above
Pleasant is the taste to the thirsting soul
Impartation of flavorful rest
Begin to understand
From peasant to queen
Pauper to prince

---

[1] *Taken from Song of Solomon 4:16*

Deep Pools

Your eyes, they terrify me
Deep pools of pure water
Cisterns churn in the depth of the gateways
Lost in the bliss of wonder
Collapsing on the inside and silent on the out
Endless dreams opened wide the doors
Desires suddenly become manifest
All I want to do is run away
To lock myself in a secluded cavern
To run from myself and my deepest desires

Fear entraps me, but my Lover will come for me still
Into the abyss, my heart goes onward
The things most precious are the things worth contending for
Unlock the treasure chest

Some things will never be comprehended in the mind
So, close tight your eyes and listen to the patter of your soul
The Spirit beats the tune you cannot deny

The fields are white and waiting for HIS fire to fall
Sent ambassadors, prepare
Render not your heart too soon
Battles won on bended knee
Conquering Lion, sing us Your victory tune

All for love
All for love
All for love
All for love
All for love

Silence

Silence

Where you hear the secrets of the dawn and bask in the caress of the wind amongst the trees

Silence

Where hope dreams and time passes on

Silence

Where you can feel the power of the earth and of the One who created it

Silence

Think now, lest you speak

Silence

Clear your mind to receive crystal clean vision once again

Silence

Before you regret, repent, lament

Silence

Afterwards and before

Silence

Feel the love flow from one heart into yours

Silence

Upbeat streets echo the agony of the day

Silence

May it cry aloud amongst the forgotten graves and graces of the yesteryears

Silence

The noise has finally begun

FIDELITY

Do we truly comprehend the nature and purpose of fidelity?
It is to live in observance and in loyalty of promises once made
It is to honor the oath we swore in our heart of hearts

How does fidelity with the Father play into our everyday existence?
It is high time to stop all the vilifying of our neighbors, friends, family, and fellow saints
The Spirit is becoming a billow within many of our own spirits
The feeling of swelling increasing
The outpour is beginning...

Release all tension and ill regard
Make your amends and forgive all
Become so real, that you may become transparent

Beauty and grace
Grace and beauty
The art of loving without old wounds
The wonder of contentment found within the everyday

Circle

Critique, define, analyze, challenge, and defend
Confined, pry, understand, and complete
Circle up, circle down
Spin

Around and around we go; where we end, no one knows
Though many think they do
Tired, exhausted, maxed out, and worn
In need of rest
Fatigue is not the enemy but the result

My own conclusion stands as such
We are morphed, confused, wrecked, selfish, and faulty beings
Therefore, we could not make it to Him on our own
Old issues resurface – the talk of the root
Here we go again…

What about simplicity?
Now, let us narrow it down here…

I'm hurt and in pain

I was wronged and allowed my guard down enough to once again be deceived

Now, you can force any answer or a reason, but mine stands as this…

Sin

We are sinful and all of us miss it

No need to constantly get to the bottom

I need to hear from Him

Straight from the throne

From Him alone

This is where my peace lies

Where it will remain…

In Him

Please don't try so hard to understand

Realize simply that I am one of man

Idiosyncrasies?

Oh, yes, I have!

Do you realize that imperfection is in us all?

You say no leader is among us except for One, but I beg to differ

We are no better than any institution

His body is found there as well as on the streets throughout the world

Whether it be Wall Street or the Bronx

Paper Mache

Laughter rings loud amongst the clanging setbacks of the day

An entourage of silhouettes press deep across the canvas of yesterday's past

A myriad of thoughts swirl inside the prophet's mind

Lightning strikes once again

Clouds of black thunder roll

Day break seems so far away yet, it is swiftly approaching

Dawn breaks forth without any sign of remorse

Paper Mache lives are quickly exposed and disposed of

Left is only a trickling of life until finally the first breath of fresh air is inhaled

How heavenly is its presence amidst the polluted darkness

Breathe it in and slowly exhale

Everything has its own rhyme, rhythm, time, space, and place

Forgotten no more, the child rises with a seemingly peculiar strength that none can take

After a while, he is soon ready to embark upon the unforgettable voyage of transitional living

Echoes of victory shouts loud and clear from the mountains to the valley

It is time!

Conquest

Conquest stolen only to begin once again
Beating drums and delicate tambourines
An ambiance of true peace fills the air

Destinies once foretold but then forgotten
They are remembered now under the shade of the ebony tree
Dragons beware... a new King has come to town
Take your temptress tongue of seduction to the lair with you
You will be chained and bound for a thousand years
Released only to be recaptured after a short time and then forever abolished
How's that for strategy!

Take the Book that has been written as your guide
Find wisdom for your life as well as for the nations
Tender warriors, rise and feel His power
Authority is yours for the taking
You were breathed upon by the Grand Author of all life

Set out a decree for His glory to sound
Set out a decree for the lost to be found
No longer a slave to the puppet master
No longer headed for darkness and disaster

Take a look deep within
Take a moment… you will find Him
Don't be distracted… keep your eyes on the prize
Hand in hand on the wings of the Dove, we rise!

Gale

Stellar lights whisper bright amidst the planets of the galaxy
Nothing made by human hands could ever compare to this

Sitting in the alcove between here and there
I hear the harp and lyre playing the sweetest melody in my mind
A transitional tune of triumph dances amongst the fallen leaves
A gale starts to rise from beneath the surface of the earth
I lie down and loll as the wind carries me up in a peaceful cyclone

If this is death or life, I cannot tell

Into the arched opening, I blaze... only to awaken in my bed's torn sheets
Vivid dreams steal my heart once more
On this journey of journeys

Show Me

Breakthrough the chaotic haze
Learn to bring forth the rays
Speak now before it is too late
Do not leave it all up to fate

Rise before the dawn of light
Know that you are still precious in His sight
Breakers, come wash me clean
Breakers, come show me what is unseen

Weary from walking in vain
Tired of hanging my head in shame
Welcome grace, come and live in me
Welcome grace, come in and set us free

Circles and circles and circles and circles
Longing for a straight line
Longing for a straight line

Guide me now
Show me how

Guide me now
Show me how

Do not leave me to wander here
Teach me to set aside my fear
Do not leave me to wander here
Teach me to set aside my fear

Rivers come and rivers go
I want to live right in Your flow
No one can help me; it's all up to You
I need endurance to wait until the time is due
I feel so broken like I'm falling apart
I may be smiling but not in my heart
Tortured by my lack of trust
I know to survive… this is a must

I place my hand in Yours to lead the way
I know in this wasteland – I cannot stay
Meant for joy
Made to bring truth
This is my desire:
Your Holy Fire

Holy Fire

Holy Fire expose the dust
Filter all the excessive waste of my soul
Define my expression
Lead me into the realm that You desire

Saints stand shoulder to shoulder marching to the beat of the warring drum
Peace is found only in their hearts and minds
Battle rages amongst them
Those who think it unreal, swiftly die
Peasants become generals, and kings become peasants
Hope ricochets from one heart to another
It is the PURPOSE that keeps them walking in stride
And love that brought them here in the first place
Attention:
All who are weak
Attention:
All who are in despair
Attention:
All who are lonely and depressed

Fix your eyes on the Glorious One
Fix your eyes, or you will never survive this war
Eyes fixed – the march continues

With visions no longer on ourselves, the pace quickens…
Onward we march, defacing the plans of the wicked one
We worry not of hunger or weariness
But only think of freedom and the coming fullness of completion

It is written…
On earth as it is in heaven
Heads bowed low – we feel the earth tremble beneath us, but no fear do we have
Fixed eyes on the prize of our Lord
Fixed eyes on the prize of our Lord

Habits

Habits we form we know not from where
Ideas become dreams that we rarely share
Painful experiences leave the heart in much sorrow
Often, it's hard to picture a bright tomorrow

How long do you hope when nothing seems to go right?
How do you battle when you don't even know who to fight?
So, a guard is built solid around the soul and the heart
No one can get in when they don't know where to start
Do you begin with a rhyme that may go unheard?
Or would the candid truth seem too absurd?

To be good with words and yet not know how to speak
To be filled with wonder on how to share the true treasure that I seek
I'm no good at hiding or pretending that I don't care

How careless I've been; I've been so unfair
Expecting a miracle without any movement
Without a first step, there's no chance of improvement
To jump off a cliff, I could very well die
But it's worth the risk if I learn how to fly

I've been given wings that I've never seen before
You have them too; just open the door
They will take you places that you've never been in your life
They'll allow you to soar far above all your strife

Life isn't easy nor is it fair
But it is a blessing and a road meant to share
To walk alone doesn't seem to be bad
But the very thought would make anyone sad
We're created beings that are made to love
We're created beings made by the One above

He writes out our stories with the quill of His pen
He'll shut the lion's mouth for you if you call from within the den
Nothing is over where new life begins
The blood washes away all the corrosion of our sins

Keep on running and never find peace
Or open your heart and experience your release
Expand your horizons like never before
Knock and you'll find Him waiting at your door

Nothing is by accident including this
There is nothing to fear except for eternal bliss
Turn your eyes away from the temporal and look deeper still
Open your spirit to His and accept your fill

Romanced by Him

I was lying there naked and barren...

Bruised and wounded beyond repair.

Alone, I silently waited for death to come; then suddenly, He was there.

He said He had been watching...

Waiting for me to cry out.

He came to me and gently picked me up.

He nursed my wounds and restored me to health.

He clothed me with splendor...

The greatest apparel I have ever seen.

He loved me...

And as He did, I could feel my heart becoming whole once again.

I fell asleep there in His arms – basking in His presence.

I was at peace.

I awoke to the most beautiful bouquet of flowers I had ever seen.

Love letters were scattered throughout the house.

He said He had to leave, but He would soon return.

Meanwhile, I was to remember night and day the love that He displayed.

For days, I was high on the experience of His love.

I read His letters repeatedly… meditating on every word.

Days slowly turned into months, months into years.

I never went looking for Him but somehow, I knew He was with me.

Eventually, I grew weary of waiting.

I began to be wooed by another.

I was given things only a queen could dream of

Yet I had no peace.

Time escaped me, and I slowly began to realize that I was no longer a beautiful young maiden.

I was becoming a worn-out old woman.

I found myself all alone.

All my former friends and lovers had gone.

I was working and laboring hard in the fields just for a mundane existence.

I thought about my first love and wondered where He had gone.

What did it matter now?

I had not been faithful as I am sure that He had been.

Then suddenly, He was there beside me once again. Instead of a look of disgust in His eyes, He was smiling... Even with laughter.

"Hello, my bride," he said. "I've been preparing for your arrival! I cannot wait to see the look upon your face when I show you all that I have in store for you. Come, let us go!"

"No, my Lord!", I cried. "You do not understand. I am not the pure and beautiful maiden you once knew. I've defiled myself with many lovers, and I've even exchanged Your splendor for these filthy rags. Please do not look upon me anymore. There are many maidens with much more grace and beauty than I shall ever possess."

"My bride, you have yet to understand. You have been bought with a price. Feel my hands, touch my side, look into my eyes, and see the tears that I have cried. I've gone to Hades and conquered death and the grave. All for you, my love… all for you. Still, I will not force my love upon you; I will you go if you will it so."

"Oh, my Lord! It is You that I love, but I have chosen to live only for myself and my own pleasures. But how I long… *long* to please You and to bring a smile to Your lips every day, my Lord. I desire to be consumed by Your love once again."

"Then come my bride and allow me to consume you with my love once again."

So, He took me into His chamber, and His banner over me was love.

He ravished me with kisses, to Him I gave my heart fully.

Everything I had; I gave, though it was nothing in comparison to what I had received.

Absolute freedom, complete joy, and overwhelming peace --

Though trials still may come, I know the One who fights my battles, and He is who I run to in times of trouble.

People still reject me and at times even look upon me with scorn, but I know it is merely temporal and soon I will be home again and will never have to leave.

Until that hour, He protects me, guides my steps, turns my mourning into joy, and places His hand around my heart so that it will never again be broken.

I don't deserve His love and could never repay Him for it.

So, I choose to live a life of worship, follow His Spirit wherever He may lead

And believe Him at His word.

This is how this peasant girl loves her mighty King.

Now praises to Him alone will I sing.

My grave clothes He took off and now I am finally free!

My greatest hope in life is that He will use me to help others see.

The past is not what matters, and your future can be bright.

If you choose to live by faith and not only by sight.

You can feel His presence too and be led by His sweet voice.

He will not force His love upon you.

It is now your choice.

You can choose your own destiny but at the end, there will be death.

Or now you can surrender all that you have left.

This is my story…

It is all I have to give.

Open your heart to Him so that you may live.

The Road Less Travelled

On the road less traveled many obstacles cloud the way.

The path is narrow as well as lonely.

But laughter beckons me from the other side.

There, they frolic with many.

Friends and family surround them.

Beautiful idols decorated in modern fashions.

They have everything…

Everything but the best.

They live for earthly pleasure, content with human gain.

Men marvel at the progress they have made.

They rise with pride at the works of their hands.

Sometimes, I wish I could be like them…

That it would be enough.

Then, I realize that the whole idea is a preposterous one.

How can I deny the life that was breathed into me?

I cannot!

I will not!

As I go, bag upon my back, a silent familiar tear slides down my cheek.

If only the path I traveled wasn't so narrow…

If only more understood.

Sometimes, it hurts to see.

But I know that it is far better than remaining blind.

Deep down, I know this to be true.

So, I go…

Walking hand in hand with my Maker.

I journey leaving behind all for the road less traveled.

Many have gone before me and many more will follow.

Perhaps, even one day, many will come all at once and the narrow way will become broad.

The time is nearing…

Change is here.

Now, I must let go of all fear.

There is a test set to purify.

May I come forth as silver.

May I shine the heart of my King as I journey the road less traveled.

Rise

Sometimes, plans go haywire, and things often don't make sense

Sometimes, I hear You speak to me and then turn around like I'm dense

Sometimes, the tears just flow, and they seem to have no end

Sometimes, I sit and wonder why You would ever choose to have me as Your friend

And then I remember a little tale that I was told so long ago…

About a heavenly Prince that came down low

A great gift of love He had to bestow

The gift has been rejected and forgotten, even by those who once cherished its treasure

If I were to admit the truth, at times, I only valued its pleasure

How ungrateful I have been, despite His precious blood

No longer holding back but boldly, I will rise to the next phase

For I was designed to bring Him the highest praise

I feel the current changing; I sense it in the air
To fly on eagle's wings once again… completely free of this world
I'd leave behind man's opinion and no longer care
Bring me to that place where it's just You and me
To that place of beauty and restoration
The place of rebirth and life

I love You, Lord
And I lift my voice to honor you

Come Home

Freedom rises where desires start to die
Consecration leads to abandonment of one's will
Forgiveness at times will equal forgetting
Striving will surely bring you swiftly to a dead end

Displays of anger?
Straight into your own vomit

Sacrifice?
Total peace

Service with joy?
Complete fulfillment

A giving heart?
A fertile land

Don't hold back yourself from others
Your voice has power to shake nations if His slightest touch is upon you

Dance with a new song
Praise the Lord the Creator of the heavens and the earth
Sovereign, above all!

What mute idol can compare to His glory?
Shine Your Light!
Let the children come
Come children, come
Come home, the fatted calf has been prepared!
It's time for harvest
It's time for an awesomely wholesome feast

Prepare the way, my Lord…
Prepare the way!
Like a flood it will come
Like a fountain of living water
Bringing freedom to all who are parched and withered

True Beauty

Streams slowly turn into rivers
Flowing coolness since the crack of dawn
Lovely lady please refrain
No need to be so profane
Did you ever notice how lost one can become in the ritual of the everyday?

Who speaks to One that is Holy?
What words can one find?
Purity and virtue are so rare
True beauty is found there

Loving memories of the refined past
Once broken, now I am whole
Once weak, now a woman of strength
Love me slowly, gently, and fully
I know You know all, and this gives me peace
I don't know nor will ever fully understand
For often I forget, I am one of man

His Time

Hope speaks beyond the dawn.

A new challenge beckons us to lay down yesterday's travesty for a peaceful embrace of today.

Miles await us just waiting to be walked.

Tears stream as we become slowly overwhelmed by the goodness of our Creator.

Dreams of the heart are now left exposed in the light of the Majestic One.

Revolutionary riders' storm by on their horses of fire,

Stripping bare the realms of complacency.

No longer am I broken, but now complete.

It all happened as it ought to have.

In His time.

Future desires, I place on the side,

Knowing that if it is to be, it will surely be.

Only in His time.

Prepare the Forces

Prepare the forces to rise against Your foe.

Prepare the forces; it's time to go!

Prepare the forces to wage war against Your foe.

Prepare the forces; it's time to go!

I'm gonna take the land You've given me.

I'm gonna take the land and declare victory.

Abba Father, what You speak shall be.

Abba Father, open Your mouth and speak for me.

Quiet Your Heart

Humbleness often begins with a stumble or fall,
Truthfulness breaks wide to forgiveness and tumbles down the wall.

Openness bubbles over to joy,
Laughter brings love to that which was once so coy.

Developed intrusion of the Spirit's cry,
Sealed upon your heart, no need to ask why.

Chosen before time ever even began to unfold,
Lost in the wonder and what is left untold.

Beauty relies upon your disguise,
Wearing no mask at all is one who is truly wise.

Unfinished business will now take place,
A move of the Shifter that cannot be traced.

Running the distance with no sweat upon the brow,
Many join in without even asking how.

You know what is right when you quiet your heart,
I know it's not everything, but it's a good start.

So, move with the dance and set your body free,
Release the tension and just allow yourself to be.

Created to bring your Father a smile,
Just rest in Him, for it will only be a little while.

The trumpet will blast its ending tune,
So, prepare your temple, the time is coming soon!

Enjoying Winter

Winter winds keep me in
Bundled up and warm inside
Leisurely baths and blissful dreams
Times of reflection and romantic passion
Fellowship and having a drink of cheer

Seasons come and seasons go
Quicker and quicker, it seems
Each one holds a grace
A fleck of its own beauty
Now time slows down
Take a deep breath in and enjoy
Spring will soon be on its way
But don't waste today
There is a treasure in each new moon
Each daybreak, new mercies will appear
Faced with my heart, I could just weep
How good He is to me
I love you Lord, for You are good

MISSING YOU

Unforgettable twists and turns,
It is on these detours that we learn.
The Sovereign One keeps us well,
Even despite some internal hell.
Longing for ones we can no longer touch,
Our hearts ache, oh so much.
To feel the embrace of a loved one gone,
We ask of the Lord for a new song.
Believing and hoping that one day we will see,
That all that has happened was meant to be.

We all veer off the chosen path of fate,
But when we cry out it's never too late.
What is wrong can be made right if we just hold on,
We will find the place where we belong.
A day worth living,
Is a day for the King.
A bell worth ringing,
Is where freedom can sing.

I know this journey is a wild one at best,
And we are constantly being put to the test.
To love each other is the best we can do,
The love of God will see us through.

Taken Away

Full of ferocious splendor

Magnificent, prized obsession

Glory streams of light

Buzzing wind of hope

Refusal of sedation

The spirit man rising… dancing once again

Spiral winds of new beginnings

Creation recognizes the wonder of our King

I see you dancing on streets of gold

Realizing the stories so long left untold

Wining and dining beside the King

Playing your guitar as you sing

Making colors throughout the sky

Taking in the marvel as you fly

Everything you've hoped for has now come true

Your smile never ceases, for you will never again be blue

Helping the Great Artist and knowing your piece in His plan

It never made sense on earth, but now you understand

That a life worth living is living only for Him

That apart from His light, all remains corroded and dim

Total peace in knowing you will see those you love one day

Until then, you rejoice as you laugh and play

No more worries

No more regrets

No more tears or silent fear

Only joy and sound love

Only goodness and wholeness for all your years

CHILD EYES

Every good church child sits quietly and piously bows

Inside wondering what it would be like to dance gayfully and sing joyfully

They don't see God as a reason for somberness but as a cause for celebration

How has such a drabness entered the doors of His sanctuary?

Peace is well and good

But loftiness is for no child of the King

Open my heart that it may beat with Yours

Whatever path You have for us, help us to walk it with pointed stride

Not wishing for someone else's path but rejoicing in our own journey

May we embrace the adventure of it all

Rise Again

Life is a dream in which you never wake.
For the love of the Lord, I try to live for His sake.
So much He has given me,
Straight from His hand.
All he asks is my love,
And to help my fellow man understand.
That though it's not easy,
Yes, sometimes it's tough.
When you live the Master's plan,
You'll always have enough.

I'm not speaking of treasures that can be stolen or fade away.
I'm speaking of eternal gifts that will always stay.
No price can be put on joy that will last,
Nothing is more freeing than forgiving the past.
We all have those moments that shame us as we fall,
If we were always perfect, life would be quite dull.
Listen to the Potter as He leads you on His way.
Don't try to fight Him; don't try to sway.
He has so many wonders in store for us all,
Just keep on rising every time you fall.

Imagine

Imagine, a heart that grows fonder everyday

Imagine, a home that takes the time to pray

Imagine, a child who knows he is loved

Imagine, a world where everyone is someone's beloved

Imagine, total peace every time you lay your head

Imagine, no regret in any words you have said

Imagine with me, a family full of love

Imagine, each one filled with the Spirit of the Dove

Imagine, a life that's lived for only His glory

Imagine, salvation being part of everyone's story

Imagine, no self-pity, no lies, and no fear

Imagine, the One who keeps safe all you hold dear

Hike

Onward I march, though I know little of where I'm going.

I only know the path I am to take.

Some sections of the trail are breezy, and I don't even break a sweat.

But many areas traverse over rough terrain.

Sometimes, it's as if I'm crawling rather than hiking the mountain in front of me.

The only way to prepare for such a journey is to begin.

Though at the beginning, I am ill prepared.

By the end, I've grown, changed, and learned more than I've ever thought possible.

I have mastered the trail.

Look

Do you notice the man standing alone shivering in the cold?

Do you stop to look; to see if he's got a story waiting to be told?

Maybe, he's an addict or just a man down on his luck

Perhaps, he's become poor after a sudden illness he was struck

Many of us have a limit before we break down

So, maybe he just reached his and ended up in your town

It's okay to stop and to look him in the eyes

It's okay to take a moment to rid yourself of your disguise

The mask of thinking you have it made

It's to you I cry out – to you I bade

Linger with him, and let his story unfold

And become more like your Maker and allow Him to mold

To mold and define you in His will alone

It's not something you can master, but it's
something you must be shown

A little bit of love will go a long way

So, give this stranger a reason to stay

Spin

The world spins 'round, and we barely keep up

Ups and downs are the flow of life

But there is so much more beyond existing

Living is found in taking hold of precious moments

Of letting them in and allowing them to imprint upon our souls

For one day, we will long for today…

To be back in this place and time

So, lavish love on your family…

For only One knows what tomorrow will bring

You Saw Me

You saw me stumble in the darkness
You held out Your hand
I saw You standing in the bright pure light
How it blinded me so, while at the same time, set me free to truly see

How Your hands: they formed the heavens
How Your hands: they formed me too
How Your hands: they took the piercing
How I love those Holy hands

Bandage up my weakness
Hold me as I go
May we walk the trail intended
Setting fires as we go

Fools Gold

Don't throw away pearls for something made of glass
Don't turn from your Maker to bow down to brass
The treasures of the fool – you know they never last
A true jewel is making beauty out of your past

So, bow to the Maker
Let Him mold you in His hands
As He sings a song of freedom, you start to understand
You're created for a purpose
Such a matchless design
He will set your pathway right and make it all align

Drink

Come to the King and be set free
Come to the Throne of Liberty
Drink from the stream that brings new life
Where mercy flows, and there's no strife
Come to the mountain and be set free
Oh, worship the King of Liberty

Sail On

Ransacked and tripled back – don't try to define
Upside down and right side up – let's make it clear again
Reason this and argue that
Let us not stay the same

The Holy Spirit is looking for a place to land
He is searching for a man to understand
Rise mighty warrior for it's time to awaken
Everything that's not of Him will be taken
Do you search for Him in the dead of night?
But when He finds you, say that you're alright?

The need for Him is a vital key
It's what opens the blind eyes to see
Once blind, naked, confused and alone
All have sat at times on a counterfeit throne
Longing for no fluffy fairytale dream
When it is on the wings of the Dove, we can truly sail

Holy Hill

There is no war at all upon His Holy Hill
Only peace abides
The streams they flow from the Living Man.
The streams bring life to all that live
Every living thing
They give the breath to all that breathe
Every living thing
To touch the stream is to touch His hand
We begin to understand
We are a piece in His great masterpiece
The Maker has a plan
For every soul, there is a place in His Holy Land.

Jesus Christ redeemed my life
He redeemed my life!
Don't run from Him
Come, jump right in!
Let His blood wash away your sin
Come, be born again!

Finding the Way Home

For many years I searched and sought out many different religions and philosophies. I didn't want the Bible to be true or Jesus to be the answer. I had been deeply hurt by a local church and hypocritical Christians. So much so that I wanted nothing to do with church, Jesus, or the Bible. I still had a deep ache and hunger for truth.

That search ultimately lead me home. Back into the arms of Jesus. My questions and wandering didn't sway His love and plan for me. He pursued me and led me back to Him.

Please don't judge a perfect God for the way a flawed human treated you. We are all desperately in need of a Savior. Thankfully He came and is now offering you, His hand. Will you take it?

What is Salvation?

We were created for a deep relationship with our Creator. God made us and loves each one of us. Unfortunately, since the first humans (Adam and Eve) we have chosen to believe lies and embrace the chaos of sin. All of us have sinned. All of us miss it and mess up at times. We live in a fallen and imperfect world. Each of us deserves the death penalty for our sins against God.

Romans 6:23 - For the wages of sin is death, but the gift of God is eternal life in Christ Jesus our Lord.

But God saw us as His beloved children and in His grace and sovereignty, bridged the chasm between us that sin caused. Jesus put on human flesh and was born of a human woman to dwell among us. He was perfect in every way. He never sinned but He died on a cross to bear the burden of our sins and take the punishment that we deserve. He died the death penalty in our place and took all our faults and imperfections to the grave with Him.

John 3:16 -For God so loved the world that he gave his one and only Son, that whoever believes in him shall not perish but have eternal life.

But on the third day, God raised Jesus from the dead. Jesus took the keys of hell and death showed us that if we belong to Him, death is not the end of the story! We can live with Him forever!

Revelation 1:18 - "I am the Living One; I was dead, and now look, I am alive for ever and ever! And I hold the keys of death and Hades."

Because of Jesus' sacrifice and resurrection, our sins can be forgiven and we can have eternal life with God!

Finding the Way

I know this is a lot to take in. But it is true. Jesus, the Son of God, left heaven to come to earth to show us the way home to God. Our eternal home is not here. We are meant to live and dwell forever with God as our Father and with Jesus in heaven. All we have to do is believe and accept that he was indeed the Messiah, the Savior of the World.

Romans 10:9-10 - If you declare with your mouth, "Jesus is Lord", and believe in your heart that God raised Him from the dead, you will be saved. For it is with your heart that you believe and are justified and it is with your mouth that you profess your faith and are saved.

If you're ready to give your life to Jesus, then just ask Him to come into your life and be Lord of your life.

If you're not ready, then please don't stop seeking. Ask God to reveal Himself to you and start by reading the Gospel of John in the Bible. As you read, ask God to speak to you. He loves you and has a mighty plan for your life. The time for salvation is now. Jesus is the way.

John 14:6 - Jesus answered, "I am the way, and the truth and the life. No one comes to the Father except through me."

Acknowledgements

I'd like to thank my parents, Ron Greene and Denice Kay, for teaching me the truth at young age. The years you spent teaching us scriptures, to put our trust in God, and the many hours at church have not been wasted. You gave us all a firm and unshakeable foundation. I'm passing the legacy on to my boys. Thank you!

I'd like to thank my wonderfully devoted husband, Josh. You believe in me even when I don't believe in myself. You see such beauty inside me and for that, I am eternally grateful. Thank you for your patience, love, and devotion. I love you so!

Jared and Jace; you are the lights of my life. "I love you more than a monkey playing a banjo. I love you more than a hippo doing ballet. I love you more than a zebra ice skating with a gecko. And I love you, love you, love you more each day."

I have been blessed with so many wonderful friends. I had a dear friend die when she was 30 years old. Her name was Melissa (Clough) Mongan. Melissa was excited about everything I wrote and such a great encouragement to me. I finally did it girl!! I wrote the book. I miss you and look forward to seeing you again.

To my other great encouragers and dear friends: Tamesa Hock, Sha'lene Boyer, Melissa Fabian, Jenn Hollinger, Jodi Hillard. (Thanks for the laptop too Jodi! 😊) I'm blessed to have you all in my life.

This book wouldn't have been possible without my publisher, Wendy Bowen. Thank you for taking a chance on me and for all the hours you put into this book coming to fruition. Also, great thanks to Sheila Kay for connecting us together.

Brian and Bud are my brothers and they have spent many, many hours writing poetry with me in our teenage years. You both inspired me to write and find my voice. Thank you.

To my lovely sisters; Kim and Annie; Thank you for always being there for me and listening to me ramble on. I'm blessed to have sisters as friends.

Time will not allow me to acknowledge all who have poured into my life. So many have touched my life and my heart. Thank you all!

Lastly, a great thanks to you the reader. I appreciate you picking up this book, giving it a chance, and hopefully letting it speak to you. BLESSINGS!

About the Author

Julie Pack's life has been re-created through her relationship with the Creator. Having been set free from the darkness of her past, she is right now in her most rewarding season of life, capturing every moment, living with gratitude, and always seeing life as an adventure. She has enjoyed ministering, traveling missions, and many years of banking. Julie currently lives and thrives in Lancaster County, PA, with her husband, Joshua, and their two energetic sons.

About Manifest Publications

Manifest Publications is the publishing division of Manifest International, LLC. Our objective is to help like-minded ministries and writers produce and distribute materials which proclaim Jesus Christ to all the world and equip the global Church for unity and maturity.

www.manifestinternational.com

www.ingramcontent.com/pod-product-compliance
Lightning Source LLC
Chambersburg PA
CBHW071955070426
42453CB00008BA/797